AF469683

Enduring Words
FOR THE
ATHLETE

The Five Mile Press

The Five Mile Press

The Five Mile Press Pty Ltd
950 Stud Road, Rowville
Victoria 3178
Australia

Email: publishing@fivemile.com.au
Website: www.fivemile.com.au

First published 2006

Compiled by Margaret Miller
Designed by Zoe Murphy

Printed in China

ISBN 1 74124 946 5

CONTENTS

PREFACE

Athletes are the heroes of modern times. In the media, they are often referred to as Olympians—as though there is something superhuman in their achievements. And perhaps there is.

Some people are undoubtedly born with the aptitude for a particular sport or athletic event. But, as the athletes represented in this anthology assert, the gifted amateur will never succeed without certain qualities of mind and attitude. These include the will to succeed, the setting of personal goals, and a willingness to work with intense determination to achieve these goals. The men and women who are quoted in this anthology speak from hard work and experience, having achieved excellence at the cost of great personal sacrifice.

The collected inspiration in *Enduring Words for the Athlete* will not only motivate dedicated athletes. It will speak to all who challenge themselves to succeed in any realm of life. For all who exemplify hard work, determination, and unremitting perseverance, this anthology celebrates your achievements.

Mind Power

$\mathcal{Y}$our mental attitude

is something you can control outright,

and you must use self-discipline

until you create a positive mental attitude –

your mental attitude attracts to you

everything that makes you what you are.

———————————

Napoleon Hill, 1883–1970
American author

Focus on remedies, not faults.

Jack Nicklaus, b. 1940
American golfer

A positive thinker

does not refuse to recognize the negative;

he refuses to dwell on it.

Positive thinking is a form of thought which

habitually looks for the best results

from the worst conditions.

Norman Vincent Peale, 1898–1993
American writer, minister

he man

who has no imagination

has no wings.

Muhammad Ali, b. 1942
American world heavyweight boxing champion

*W*isdom is always

an overmatch for strength.

Phil Jackson, b. 1945
American basketball coach

*A*bility

is what you're capable of doing.

Motivation

determines what you do.

Attitude

determines how well you do it.

Lou Holtz, b. 1937
American college football coach

*N*ever underestimate the power of dreams

and the influence of the human spirit.

We are all the same in this notion:

The potential for greatness

lives within each of us.

Wilma Rudolph, 1940–1994
American Olympic athlete, runner

Adventure isn't hanging on a rope

off the side of a mountain.

Adventure is an attitude that we must apply

to the day to day obstacles of life –

facing new challenges,

seizing new opportunities,

testing our resources against the unknown

and, in the process, discovering

our own unique potential.

John Amatt, b. 1945
English mountaineer

The most important facets of golf

are careful planning,

calm and clear thinking,

and the ordinary logic

of common sense.

—————————————

Peter Thomson, b. 1929
Australian golfer

Shoulda, coulda, and woulda

won't get it done.

In attacking adversity,

only a positive attitude, alertness,

and regrouping to basics

can launch a comeback.

Pat Riley, b. 1945
American basketball coach

*T*he greatest revolution of our generation

is the discovery that human beings,

by changing the inner attitudes of their minds,

can change the outer aspects of their lives.

William James, 1842–1910
American psychologist, philosopher

*I never looked at the consequences
of missing a big shot ....
When you think about the consequences,
you always think of a negative result.*

Michael Jordan, b. 1963
American basketball player

Champions aren't made in gyms.

Champions are made from

something they have deep inside them:

a desire, a dream, a vision.

They have to have last minute stamina;

they have to be a little faster;

they have to have the skill and the will.

But the will must be stronger than the skill.

Muhammad Ali, b. 1942
American world heavyweight boxing champion

*Striving for excellence
motivates you;
striving for perfection
is demoralizing.*

Harriet Braiker, 1949–2004
American author

You are what you think.

You are what you go for.

You are what you do!

Bob Richards, b. 1926
American Olympic athlete, pole vaulter, runner

What distinguishes
certain players from others
is the mental aspect.

Michael Jordan, b. 1963
American basketball player

Every memorable act in the history of the world

is a triumph of enthusiasm.

Nothing great was achieved without it

because it gives any challenge or any occupation,

no matter how frightening or difficult, a new meaning.

Without enthusiasm, you are doomed

to a life of mediocrity, but with it,

you can accomplish miracles.

Og Mandino, 1923–1996
American author

Find the good.

It's all around you.

Find it, showcase it,

and you'll start believing it.

Jesse Owens, 1913–1980
American Olympic athlete, runner

People do not lack strength;

they lack will.

Victor Hugo, 1802–1885
French writer, poet

I don't think of myself

as a poor, deprived ghetto girl

who made good.

I think of myself

as somebody who from an early age

knew I was responsible for myself,

and I had to make good.

Oprah Winfrey, b. 1954
American television personality

*V*enus told me the other day that champions

don't get nervous in tight situations.

That really helped me a lot.

I decided I shouldn't get nervous

and to just do the best I can.

Serena Williams, b. 1981
American tennis player

Strength does not come

from physical capacity.

It comes from

an indomitable will.

Mahatma Gandhi, 1869–1948
Indian political leader

*The difference
between winning and losing
is always a mental one.*

Peter Thomson, b. 1929
Australian golfer

$\mathcal{I}$ try to concentrate

on concentrating.

Martina Navratilova, b. 1956
Czech-born American tennis player

*T*he difference between

a successful person and others

is not a lack of strength,

not a lack of knowledge,

but rather a lack of will.

Vince Lombardi, 1913–1970
American football coach

What counts is not necessarily

the size of the dog in the fight –

it's the size of the fight

in the dog.

Dwight D. Eisenhower, 1890–1969
President of the United States of America

I always felt that my greatest asset

was not my physical ability;

it was my mental ability.

Bruce Jenner, b. 1949
American Olympic athlete, runner

I am the toughest golfer mentally.

Tiger Woods, b. 1975
American golfer

*I*f you can believe it,

the mind can achieve it.

Ronnie Lott, b. 1959
American football player

Set Goals

$\mathscr{S}$hoot for the moon.

Even if you miss it,

you will land among the stars.

Lester Louis Brown, b. 1928
American journalist

If you set a goal for yourself

and are able to achieve it,

you have won your race.

Your goal can be to come in first,

to improve your performance,

or just finish the race —

it's up to you.

Dave Scott, b.1954
American triathlete, six-time ironman world champion

I always wanted to be

the best I could be at whatever I did.

I didn't want to be the number one golfer in the world.

I just wanted to be as good as I could be.

Greg Norman, b. 1955
Australian golfer

*I*t is better to look ahead and prepare

than to look back and regret.

Jackie Joyner-Kersee, b. 1962
American Olympic athlete, track and field

*I*f you aspire to the highest place,

it is no disgrace to stop at the second

or even the third place.

Cicero, 106–43 BC
Roman orator, statesman, essayist

Achievement is largely the product

of steadily raising one's level

of aspiration and expectation.

Jack Nicklaus, b. 1940
American golfer

*You are never too old

to set another goal or to

dream a new dream.*

C. S. Lewis, 1898–1963
English writer, scholar

You've got to try and
reach for the stars or try
and achieve the unreachable.

Cathy Freeman, b. 1973
Australian Olympic athlete, track

*You don't have to be a fantastic hero
to do certain things – to compete.
You can be just an ordinary chap,
sufficiently motivated to
reach challenging goals.*

Sir Edmund Hillary, b. 1919
New Zealand mountaineer

$\mathcal{D}$on't be afraid of the space

between your dreams and reality.

If you can dream it,

you can make it so.

Belva David, b. 1932
American journalist

*M*y ability to concentrate
and work toward that goal
has been my greatest asset.

Jack Nicklaus, b. 1940
American golfer

The reason most people

never reach their goals

is that they don't define them,

learn about them, or even seriously

consider them as believable or achievable.

Winners can tell you where they are going,

what they plan to do along the way,

and who will be sharing

the adventure with them.

Denis Waitley, b. 1933
American productivity consultant

Our aspirations

are our possibilities.

Samuel Johnson, 1709–1784
English lexicographer, critic, essayist

Far away, there in the sunshine,

are my highest aspirations.

I may not reach them,

but I can look up and see their beauty,

believe in them,

and try to follow them.

Louisa May Alcott, 1832–1888
American novelist

$\mathcal{Y}$ou have to learn the rules of the game.

And then you have to play the game

better than anyone else.

Albert Einstein, 1879–1955
German-born American physicist

The most important thing

about motivation

is goal-setting.

You should always have a goal.

Francie Larrieu Smith, b. 1952
American Olympic athlete, track and field

$\mathcal{W}$hen a thing is done, it's done.

Don't look back.

Look forward to your next objective.

George C. Marshall, 1880–1959
American general

The achievement of one goal

should be the

starting point of another.

Alexander Graham Bell, 1847–1922
Scottish-born American inventor

$\mathcal{T}$he world makes way for the man

who knows where he is going.

Ralph Waldo Emerson, 1803–1882
American poet, essayist, teacher

Sheer Hard Work

$\mathcal{I}$’ve always believed

that if you put in the work,

the results will come.

I don’t do things half-heartedly

because I know if I do,

then I can expect half-hearted results.

Michael Jordan, b. 1963
American basketball player

*N*obody's a natural.

You work hard to get good

and then work to get better.

It's hard to stay on top.

Paul Coffey, b. 1961
Canadian ice hockey player

Champions keep playing until they get it right.

Billie Jean King, b. 1943
American tennis player

$\mathcal{I}$'m a great believer in luck,

and I find the harder I work,

the more I have of it.

Thomas Jefferson, 1743–1826
President of the United States of America

$\mathcal{A}$ dictionary is the only place

where success comes before work.

Hard work is the price we must pay for success.

I think you can accomplish anything

if you're willing to pay the price.

Vince Lombardi, 1913–1970
American football coach

The harder you work,

the harder it is

to surrender.

Vince Lombardi, 1913–1970
American football coach

$\mathcal{Y}$ou are

what you repeatedly do.

Excellence is not an event –

it is a habit.

—————————————

Aristotle, 384–322 BC
Greek philosopher

*Start early

and begin raising the bar

throughout the day.*

Bruce Jenner, b. 1949
American Olympic athlete, runner

$\mathcal{Y}$ou owe it to yourself

to be the best you can possibly be –

in baseball and in life.

Pete Rose, b. 1941
American baseball player

Good, better, best,

May you never rest

Until your good is better

And your better best.

———

Anonymous

When we do the best we can,

we never know what miracle

is wrought in our life

or the life of another.

Helen Keller, 1880–1968
American writer, lecturer

$\mathcal{T}o$ give anything less than your best

is to sacrifice the gift.

Steve Roland Prefontaine, 1951–1975
American distance runner

*I*t takes a struggle,

a goal, and enthusiasm

to make a champion.

Norman Vincent Peale, 1898–1993
American writer, minister

You miss 100 percent

of the shots you never take.

Wayne Gretzky, b. 1961
Canadian-born ice hockey player

Nobody

who ever gave his best

regretted it.

George Halas, 1895–1983
American football coach

*M*ost people never run

far enough on their first wind

to find out they've got a second.

____

William James, 1842–1910
American psychologist, philosopher

I do the very best I know how –

the very best I can;

and I mean to keep on doing it

until the end.

Abraham Lincoln, 1809–1865
President of the United States of America

*I*f you train hard,

you'll not only be hard,

you'll be hard to beat.

Herschel Walker, b. 1962
American baseball player

$\mathcal{D}$urability is part of

what makes a great athlete.

Bill Russell, b. 1934
American basketball player

That which does not kill me

makes me stronger.

Friedrich Nietzsche, 1844–1900
German philosopher

*C*onfidence is the most important

single factor in this game,

and no matter how great your natural talent,

there is only one way

to obtain and sustain it: Work.

Jack Nicklaus, b. 1940
American golfer

I learned that the only way

you are going to get anywhere in life

is to work hard at it.

Whether you're a musician, a writer,

an athlete, or a businessman,

there is no getting around it.

If you do, you'll win.

If you don't, you won't.

Bruce Jenner, b. 1949
American Olympic athlete, runner

Continuous effort – not strength

or intelligence – is the key

to unlocking our potential.

Sir Winston Churchill, 1874–1965
British Prime Minister, statesman, writer

I'm trying as hard as I can,

and sometimes things don't go my way,

and that's the way things go.

Tiger Woods, b. 1975
American golfer

The man who removes a mountain begins by carrying away small stones.

William Faulkner, 1897–1962
American novelist

A winner is someone

who recognizes his God-given talents,

works his tail off to develop them into skills,

and uses these skills to accomplish his goals.

Larry Bird, b. 1956
American basketball player

I know the price of success:

dedication, hard work,

and an unremitting devotion

to the things you want to see happen.

Frank Lloyd Wright, 1867–1959
American architect

*L*uck has nothing to do with it –

because I have spent many, many hours,

countless hours, on the court

working for my one moment in time

not knowing when it would come.

Serena Williams, b. 1981
American tennis player

I wasn't always a terrific athlete.

I can remember times

when I couldn't run, jump,

and chew gum at the same time.

And I just had to practice, practice, practice.

I became a pretty good athlete

after hard work.

Shaquille O'Neal, b. 1972
American basketball player

The difference between
the impossible and the possible
lies in a person's determination.

Tommy Lasorda, b. 1927
American baseball manager

*D*on't let the best you have done so far

be the standard for the rest of your life.

Gustavus F. Swift, 1839–1903
American business magnate

*L*eaders are made; they are not born.

They are made by hard effort,

which is the price which all of us

must pay to achieve

any goal that is worthwhile.

Vince Lombardi, 1913–1970
American football coach

There is a better way to do it;

find it.

Thomas A. Edison, 1847–1931
American inventor

$\mathscr{A}$ll right Mister,

let me tell you what winning means ….

You're willing to go longer, work harder,

give more than anyone else.

Vince Lombardi, 1913–1970
American football coach

On the mountains of truth,

you can never climb in vain:

Either you will reach a point higher up today,

or you will be training your powers so that

you will be able to climb higher tomorrow.

Friedrich Nietzche, 1844–1900
German philosopher, poet

Believe in Yourself

Some people say I have an attitude.

Maybe I do. But I think you have to.

You have to believe in yourself

when no one else does —

that makes you a winner right there.

Venus Williams, b. 1980
American tennis player

*I*t's lack of faith

that makes people afraid

of meeting challenges,

and I believe in myself.

Muhammad Ali, b. 1942
American world heavyweight boxing champion

*E*very achiever that I have ever met says,

'My life turned around

when I began to believe in me.'

Dr. Robert Schuller, b. 1926
American minister

You have to expect things of yourself before you can do them.

Michael Jordan, b. 1963
American basketball player

My mother taught me very early

to believe I could achieve

any accomplishment I wanted to.

The first was to walk without braces.

Wilma Rudolph, 1940–1995
American Olympic athlete, runner

$\mathcal{T}$he better I get,

the more I realize

how much better I can get.

Martina Navratilova, b. 1956
Czech-born American tennis player

You can do what you have to do,

and sometimes you can do it

even better than you think you can.

Jimmy Carter, b. 1924
President of the United States of America

$\mathcal{T}$hey can

because they think they can.

Virgil, 70–9 BC
Roman poet

Have patience with all things,

but chiefly have patience with yourself.

Do not lose courage in considering

your own imperfections,

but instantly set about remedying them —

every day begin the task anew.

St. Francis de Sales, 1567–1622
French ecclesiastic

*A*nything is possible.

You can be told that you have a 90 percent chance

or a 50 percent chance or a 1 percent chance,

but you have to believe,

and you have to fight.

Lance Armstrong, b. 1971
American champion cyclist

*I*t's hard to be humble

when you're as great as I am.

Muhammad Ali, b. 1942
American world heavyweight boxing champion

*N*ever bend your head.

Always hold it high.

Look the world right in the eye.

Helen Keller, 1880–1968
American writer, lecturer

$\mathcal{B}$eyond a wholesome discipline,

be gentle with yourself.

You are a child of the universe,

no less than the trees or the stars;

you have a right to be here.

Max Ehrmann, 1872–1945
American poet

I realized from a very early age

that God gave me a gift,

and that gift was to run,

and I wanted to use it to the

best of my ability.

Betty Cuthbert, b. 1938
Australian Olympic athlete, track

In my mind, I'm always the best.

If I walk out on the court

and I think the next person is better,

I've already lost.

Venus Williams, b. 1980
American tennis player

$\mathcal{N}$othing great has ever been achieved

except by those who dared believe

something inside them

was superior to circumstances.

Bruce Fairchild Barton, 1886–1967
American advertising executive, author

The thing always happens

that you really believe in;

and the belief in a thing

makes it happen.

Frank Lloyd Wright, 1869–1959
American architect

*O*ne of the greatest of all principles

is that men can do

what they think they can do.

Norman Vincent Peale, 1898–1993
American writer, minister

*T*o accomplish great things,

we must not only act,

but also dream;

not only plan,

but also believe.

Anatole France, 1844–1924
French writer, poet

*Whether you believe
you can do a thing
or believe you can't,
you are right.*

Henry Ford, 1863–1947
American automobile manufacturer

$\mathcal{B}$elieve you can, and you can.

Belief is one of the most powerful

of all problem dissolvers.

When you believe that a difficulty

can be overcome, you are more than halfway

to victory over it already.

Norman Vincent Peale, 1898–1993
American writer, minister

Healthy in Mind and Body

$\mathcal{P}$hysical fitness is not only one of the

most dynamic keys to a healthy body,

it is the basis of dynamic

and creative intellectual activity.

John F. Kennedy, 1917–1963
President of the United States of America

Of course, I want to be number one.

But being happy and healthy

is the most important thing.

Venus Williams, b. 1980
American tennis player

Your prayers should be

for a healthy mind

in a healthy body.

Juvenal, c. 60–130

Roman poet, stoic

*It is not to live
but to be healthy
that makes a life.*

Martial, c. 40–104 AD
Roman poet

A man too busy

to take care of his health

is like a mechanic too busy

to take care of his tools.

———

Anonymous

*H*ealth is the greatest of all possessions;

a hale cobbler is better

than a sick king.

Jonathan Swift, 1667–1745
Irish satirist, essayist, cleric

Walking is the best possible exercise.

Habituate yourself to walk very far.

Thomas Jefferson, 1743–1826
President of the United States of America

Take care of your body with steadfast fidelity.

The soul must see through these eyes alone,

and if they are dim,

the whole world is clouded.

____

Johann Wolfgang von Goethe, 1749–1832
German poet, writer, scientist

The scientific truth

may be put quite briefly:

Eat moderately,

having an ordinary mixed diet,

and don't worry.

Robert Hutchinson, 1871–1960
British medical writer

Take care of your body.

It's the only place you have to live.

————

Anonymous

The preservation of health is a duty.

Few seem conscious

that there is such a thing

as physical morality.

Herbert Spencer, 1820–1903
English philosopher, journalist

$\mathcal{L}$ook to your health; and if you have it,

praise God, and value it next to a good conscience;

for health is the second blessing

that we mortals are capable of –

a blessing that money cannot buy.

Izaak Walton, 1593–1683
English writer

$\mathcal{T}$o wish to be well

is part of becoming well.

Seneca, 4 BC–65 AD

Roman dramatist, philosopher, statesman

$\mathcal{T}$rue enjoyment comes from

activity of the mind

and exercise of the body;

the two are united.

Alexander von Humboldt, 1769–1859
German scientist, explorer, writer

O health!

Health is the blessing of the rich!

The riches of the poor!

Who can buy thee at too dear a rate

since there is no enjoying this world

without thee?

Ben Jonson, 1573–1637
English dramatist, poet

Cheerfulness

is the best promoter of health

and is as friendly to the mind

as to the body.

Joseph Addison, 1672–1719
English essayist

Walking is a man's best medicine.

Hippocrates, c. 460–377 BC
Greek physician

Winning and Losing

You can't win

unless you learn how to lose.

Kareem Abdul-Jabbar, b. 1947
American basketball player

*I*f you can react the same way

to winning and losing,

that's a big accomplishment ….

Quality is important because it

stays with you the rest of your life.

Chris Evert Lloyd, b. 1954
American tennis player

*I*f you don't try to win,

you might as well hold the Olympics

in somebody's back yard.

The thrill of competing carries with it

the thrill of a gold medal.

One wants to win

to prove himself the best.

Jesse Owens, 1913–1980
American Olympic athlete, runner

When you lose,

you're more motivated.

When you win,

you fail to see your mistakes

and probably no one

can tell you anything.

Venus Williams, b. 1980
American tennis player

Why did I want to win?

Because I didn't want to lose!

The most important thing in the Olympic Games

is not winning but taking part;

the essential thing in life is not conquering

but fighting well.

Pierre de Coubertin, 1863–1937
French founder of the modern Olympic Games

Winning is not everything,

but wanting to win is.

Vince Lombardi, 1913–1970
American football coach

You're not obligated to win.

You're obligated to keep trying

to do the best you can every day.

Marian Wright Edelman, b. 1939
American attorney, civil rights activist

*L*et me win,

but if I cannot win,

let me be brave in the attempt.

———————————

Special Olympics motto

If I put everything into it,

I can't lose.

I mightn't win in terms of gold medals,

but I will win my own personal battle.

And that's what it's all about.

Ian Thorpe, b. 1982
Australian Olympic athlete, swimmer

*T*he man who can drive himself further

once the effort gets painful

is the man who will win.

Roger Bannister, b. 1929
English Olympic athlete, runner

Nice guys finish last.

Leo Durocher, 1906–1991
American baseball player, manager

The greatest memory for me

of the 1984 Olympics

was not the individual honors,

but the standing on the podium

with my team mates

to receive our team gold medal.

Mitch Gaylord, b. 1961
American Olympic athlete, gymnast

Winning is not a sometime thing,

it's an all the time thing.

You don't win once in a while,

you don't do things right once in a while,

you do them right all the time.

Winning is habit.

Unfortunately, so is losing.

Vince Lombardi, 1913–1970
American football coach

Strength does not come from winning.

Your struggles develop your strengths.

When you go through hardships

and decide not to surrender,

that is strength.

Arnold Schwarzenegger, b. 1947
German-born American actor, politician

Never Give Up!

*I*f you're trying to achieve,

there will be roadblocks.

I've had them;

everybody has had them.

But obstacles don't have to stop you.

If you run into a wall,

don't turn around and give up.

Find out how to climb it, go through it,

or work around it.

Michael Jordan, b. 1963
American basketball player

$\mathcal{D}$o not let what you cannot do
interfere with what you can do.

John Wooden, b. 1910
American basketball coach

Giving up

was never an option.

Lance Armstrong, b. 1971
American champion cyclist

Nothing in the world

can take the place of persistence.

Talent will not; nothing is more common

than unsuccessful men with talent.

Genius will not;

unrewarded genius is almost a proverb.

Education alone will not;

the world is full of educated derelicts.

Persistence and determination alone are omnipotent.

———————————————

John Calvin Coolidge, 1872–1933
President of the United States of America

$\mathcal{M}$y motto was always to keep swinging.

Whether I was in a slump

or feeling badly or having trouble off the field,

the only thing to do was to keep swinging.

———

Hank Aaron, b. 1934
American baseball player

When you get into a tight place,

and everything goes against you till it seems as though

you could not hang on a minute longer,

never give up then for that is just the place and time

that the tide will turn.

Harriet Beecher Stowe, 1811–1896
American author, social reformer

We have two options in life

both medically and emotionally:

Give up or fight like hell.

Lance Armstrong, b. 1971
American champion cyclist

*N*ever walk away from failure.

On the contrary,

study it carefully – and imaginatively –

for its hidden assets.

—————————————

Michael Korda, b. 1933
English publisher

*A*ustere perseverance,

harsh and continuous,

may be employed by the least of us,

and rarely fails of its purpose,

for its silent power grows

irreversibly greater with time.

Johann Wolfgang von Goethe, 1749–1832
German writer, scientist

I can accept failure,

but I can't accept not trying.

Michael Jordan, b. 1963
American basketball player

$\mathcal{P}$atience and perseverance

have a magical effect

before which difficulties disappear

and obstacles vanish.

John Quincy Adams, 1767–1848
President of the United States of America

I become a happier man

each time I suffer.

Lance Armstrong, b. 1971
American champion cyclist

Winners never quit

and quitters never win.

Vince Lombardi, 1913–1970
American football coach

I ran and ran and ran every day,

and I acquired this sense of determination,

this sense of spirit that I would never, never give up,

no matter what else happened.

Wilma Rudolph, 1940–1994
American Olympic athlete, runner

$\mathcal{E}$ndurance is one of

the most difficult disciplines,

but it is to the one who endures

that the final victory comes.

Guatama Siddharta, 563–483 BC
Indian founder of Buddhism

The secret of success

is constancy to purpose.

Benjamin Disraeli, 1804–1881
English statesman, writer

*E*ndurance is nobler than strength,

and patience than beauty.

―――――――――

John Ruskin, 1819–1900
English writer, critic

I've missed more than 9000 shots in my career.

I've lost almost 300 games.

26 times, I've been trusted to make the

winning game shot and missed.

I've failed over and over and over again in my life.

And that is why I succeed.

Michael Jordan, b. 1963
American basketball player

$\mathcal{E}$ndurance is the crowning quality,

and patience all the passion

of great hearts.

James Russell Lowell, 1819–1891
American poet, critic, essayist, diplomat

The quality of a person's life

is in direct proportion to

their commitment to excellence

regardless of their chosen

field of endeavor.

—

Vince Lombardi, 1913–1970
American football coach

$\mathscr{E}$ndurance

is patience

concentrated.

Thomas Carlyle, 1795–1881
Scottish historian, essayist

$\mathcal{L}$et me tell you the secret

that has led me to my goal:

My strength lies solely

in my tenacity.

Louis Pasteur, 1822–1895
French scientist

Champions keep playing

until they get it right.

Billie Jean King, b. 1943
American tennis player

When you come to the end of your rope,

tie a knot and hang on.

Franklin D. Roosevelt, 1882–1945
President of the United States of America

*I*t's not that I'm so smart,

it's just that I

stay with problems longer.

Albert Einstein, 1879–1955
German-born American physicist

$\mathscr{C}$onsider the postage stamp:

Its usefulness consists

in the ability to stick to one thing

till it gets there.

Josh Billings, 1818–1885
American humorist

*G*reat works are performed

not by strength,

but by perseverance.

Samuel Johnson, 1709–1784
English lexicographer, critic, essayist

Character consists of

what you do

on the third and fourth tries.

James A. Michener, 1907–1997
American writer

A resolute determination

is the truest wisdom.

Napoleon Bonaparte, 1769–1821
French emperor, general

If you really want something,

work hard, take advantage of opportunities,

and never give up;

you will find a way.

Jane Goodall, b. 1934
English anthropologist

*F*ight one more round.

When your arms are so tired that you

can hardly lift your hands to come on guard,

fight one more round.

When your nose is bleeding and your eyes are black

and you are so tired that you wish your opponent

would crack you one on the jaw and put you to sleep,

fight one more round –

remembering that the man who always

fights one more round

is never whipped.

James Corbett, 1866–1933
American heavyweight boxing champion

I think a hero

is an ordinary individual

who finds strength

to persevere and endure

in spite of overwhelming obstacles.

Christopher Reeve, 1952–2004
American actor

$\mathscr{A}$bility may get you to the top,

but it takes character

to keep you there.

———————

John Wooden, b. 1910
American basketball coach

I do not think there is any other quality

so essential to success of any kind

as the quality of perseverance.

It overcomes almost everything,

even nature.

John D. Rockefeller, 1839–1937
American industrialist, philanthropist

*S*tep by step,

the ladder is ascended.

George Herbert, 1593–1633
German writer, scientist

Resolve never to quit,

never to give up,

no matter what the situation.

Jack Nicklaus, b. 1940
American golfer

We didn't lose the game;

we just ran out of time.

____

Vince Lombardi, 1913–1970
American football coach

*I*n the confrontation

between the stream and the rock,

the stream always wins –

not through strength

but by perseverance.

H. Jackson Brown, b. 1948
American singer–songwriter

$\mathcal{P}$erseverance is not a long race;

it is many short races

one after another.

Walter Elliott, 1888–1958
British politician

Only a man who knows

what it is like to be defeated

can reach down to the bottom of his soul and

come up with the extra ounce of power it takes

to win when the match is even.

———————

Muhammad Ali, b. 1942
American world heavyweight boxing champion

*N*ever give in.

Never give in.

Never, never, never,

never give in.

Sir Winston Churchill, 1874-1965
British Prime Minister, statesman, writer

I have lost this battle,
but I will win the war.

Anna Kournikova, b. 1981
Russian-born tennis player

My greatest point is my persistence.

I never give up in a match.

However down I am, I fight until the last ball.

My list of matches shows that I have turned

a great many so-called irretrievable

defeats into victories.

Bjorn Borg, b. 1956
Swedish tennis player

Our greatest glory

is not in never falling,

but in rising every time we fall.

Confucius, c. 550–478 BC
Chinese philosopher

*H*e's no failure.

He's not dead yet.

Gwilym Lloyd George, 1894–1967
Welsh politician

Reflections of Athletes

$\mathcal{A}$s you walk down the fairway of life

you must smell the roses,

for you only get to play one round.

Ben Hogan, 1912–1997
American golfer

$\mathcal{I}$ gave it my body and mind,

but I have kept my soul.

Phil Jackson, b. 1945
American basketball coach

Just play.

Have fun.

Enjoy the game.

Michael Jordan, b. 1963
American basketball player

$\mathcal{D}$on't look back.

Something might be gaining on you.

Satchel Paige, 1906–1982
American baseball player

Tennis

is a perfect combination

of violent action

taking place in an atmosphere

of total tranquillity.

Billie Jean King, b. 1943
American tennis player

$\mathcal{D}$o you know

what my favorite part

of the game is?

The opportunity to play.

Mike Singletary, b. 1958
American football player

People ask me what was going through my mind in the race, and I don't know. I try and let my body do what it knows.

Ian Thorpe, b. 1982
Australian Olympic athlete, swimmer

$\mathcal{A}$pproach the game

with no preset agendas,

and you'll probably come away

surprised at your overall efforts.

———————————

Phil Jackson, b. 1945
American basketball coach

$\mathcal{T}$he moment of victory

is much too short

to live for that

and nothing else.

———————————————

Martina Navratilova, b. 1956
Czech-born American tennis player

If you can't laugh at yourself,

then who can you laugh at?

Tiger Woods, b. 1975
American golfer

There are three important things in life:

family, religion,

and the Green Bay Rollers.

Vince Lombardi, 1913–1970
American football coach

*T*o anyone who has

started out on a long campaign

believing that the gold medal

was destined for him,

the feeling when, all of a sudden,

the medal has gone somewhere else

is quite indescribable.

Sebastian Coe, b. 1956
British Olympic athlete, runner

I've always felt

it was not up to anyone else

to make me give my best.

Akeem Olajuwon, b. 1963
Nigerian-born American basketball player

*I*t is the inspiration of the Olympic Games

that drives people not only to compete,

but to improve and to bring lasting

spiritual and moral benefits to the athlete

and inspiration to those lucky enough

to witness the athletic dedication.

Herb Elliott, b. 1938
Australian Olympic athlete, runner

*A*lways keep an open mind

and a compassionate heart.

Phil Jackson, b. 1945
American basketball coach

*T*he pitcher has got only a ball.

I've got a bat.

So the percentage in weapons is in

my favor, and I let the fellow

with the ball do the fretting.

Hank Aaron, b. 1934
American baseball player

Just go out there

and do what you have to do.

Martina Navratilova, b. 1956
Czech-born American tennis player

The way a team plays as a whole

determines its success.

You may have the greatest bunch

of individual stars in the world,

but if they don't play together,

the club won't be worth a dime.

Babe Ruth, 1895–1948
American baseball player

*A*sk not what

your team mates

can do for you.

Ask what you can do

for your team mates.

Magic Johnson, b. 1959
American basketball player

How people keep correcting us

when we are young!

There is always some bad habit or other

they tell us we ought to get over.

Yet most bad habits are tools

to help us get through life.

Jack Nicklaus, b. 1940
American golfer

A golf course should be a bit wild,

at least in some corners.

A weed now and again

would be a great relief.

———————————

Peter Thomson, b. 1929
Australian golfer

I have only one superstition.

I make sure I touch all bases

when I hit a home run.

Babe Ruth, 1895–1948
American baseball player

I get to play golf for a living.

What more can you ask for –

getting paid

for doing what you love?

Tiger Woods, b. 1975
American golfer

One chance

is all you need.

Jesse Owens, 1913–1980
American Olympic athlete, runner

For the younger sisters,

we always look up to the older sisters

because they're always ahead

of us and they always win.

Serena Williams, b. 1981
American tennis player

I always like to win.

But I'm the big sister.

I want to make sure she has everything,

even if I don't have anything.

It's hard.

I love her so much.

Venus Williams, b. 1980
American tennis player

$\mathcal{I}$'m hoping someday

that some kid, black or white,

will hit more home runs than myself.

Whoever it is,

I'd be pulling for him.

Hank Aaron, b. 1934
American baseball player

$\mathcal{B}$e bold.

If you're going to make an error,

make a doozy,

and don't be afraid to hit the ball.

Billie Jean King, b. 1943
American tennis player

Don't let

the fear of striking out

hold you back.

Babe Ruth, 1895–1948
American baseball player

I skate where the puck is going to be, not where it has been.

Wayne Gretzky, b. 1961
Canadian-born ice hockey player

A team championship doesn't happen

because three people score tens;

it happens because all the guys score well.

In my opinion, everyone deserved tens;

we're all tens on this team.

Mitch Gaylord, b. 1961
American Olympic athlete, gymnast

Guessing what the pitcher

is going to throw

is 80 percent

of being a successful hitter.

The other 20 percent

is just execution.

Hank Aaron, b. 1934
American baseball player

I don't care about numbers, man.

I just want to win basketball games.

Andrew Bogut, b. 1984
American-based Australian basketball player

What do I think about

when I strike out?

I think about hitting home runs.

The time your game is most vulnerable

is when you're ahead.

Never let up.

——————————
Rod Laver, b. 1938
Australian tennis player

*An athlete has

such a narrow view of life;

he does not know reality.*

Bruce Jenner, b. 1949
American Olympic athlete, decathlon

No one automatically gives you respect

just because you show up.

You have to earn it.

Lance Armstrong, b. 1971
American champion cyclist

$\mathcal{A}$ buoyant,

positive approach to the game

is as basic as a sound swing.

Tony Lema, 1934–1966
American golfer

*I*t's hard not to play golf

that's up to Jack Nicklaus standards

when you are Jack Nicklaus.

—————

Jack Nicklaus, b. 1940
American golfer

$\mathcal{U}$se your brain

not your endurance.

Peter Thomson, b. 1929
Australian golfer

The greatest stimulator

to my running career

was fear.

Herb Elliott, b. 1938
Australian Olympic athlete, runner

I hold it more important

to have the players' confidence

than their affection.

Vince Lombardi, 1913–1970
American football coach

$\mathcal{D}$uring our lives,

we are faced with so many elements as well;

we experience so many setbacks

and fight such a hand-to-hand battle with failure,

head down in the rain,

just trying to stay upright and have a little hope.

The Tour isn't just a bike race;

it tests you mentally, physically,

and even morally.

Lance Armstrong, b. 1971
American champion cyclist

One man can be

a crucial ingredient on a team,

but one man

cannot make a team.

Kareem Abdul-Jabbar, b. 1947
American basketball player

I won't be happy until we have

every boy in America between

the ages of six and sixteen

wearing a glove and swinging a bat.

Babe Ruth, 1895–1948
American baseball player

A light, tender,

sensitive touch

is worth a ton of brawn.

Peter Thomson, b. 1929
Australian golfer

*M*y dad always taught me these words:

Care and share.

That's why we put on clinics.

The only thing I can do is try to give back.

If it works, it works.

Tiger Woods, b. 1975
American golfer

I'm a firm believer in the theory that people only do their best at things they enjoy. It is difficult to excel at something you don't enjoy.

Jack Nicklaus, b. 1940
American golfer

$\mathcal{T}$he bigger they are,

the further they have to fall.

Bob Fitzsimmons, 1863–1917
British triple world boxing champion

$\mathcal{F}$loat like a butterfly.

Sting like a bee.

———————————

Muhammad Ali, b. 1942
American world heavyweight boxing champion

*I*t's not so important
who starts the game
but who finishes it.

John Wooden, b. 1910
American basketball coach

I guess I was probably the first woman

to lift weights and do circuit training

and to run the sand hills.

Margaret Court, b. 1942
Australian tennis player

$\mathcal{T}$he secret of my success

was clean living

and a fast outfield.

Lefty Gomez, b. 1908
American baseball player

All ball players should quit

when it starts to feel

as if the baselines run up hill.

Babe Ruth, 1895–1948
American baseball player

Sport is cut and dried.

You always know when you succeed ….

You are not an actor: You don't wonder,

'Did my performance go down alright?'

You've lost.

Steve Davis, b. 1957
English snooker player

*T*he truth is, if you asked me to choose

between winning the Tour de France and cancer,

I would choose cancer.

Odd as it sounds, I would rather have the title

of cancer survivor than winner of the Tour,

because of what it has done for me as a human being,

a man, a husband, a son, and a father.

Lance Armstrong, b. 1971
American champion cyclist

It's been a journey

for women of color, for my family.

It's one dream coming true after another.

Venus Williams, b. 1980
American tennis player

*L*earn to compartmentalize yourself.

You're an athlete for only a few more years.

You have to live 80 or 90 years,

so you better find more things to do.

Tom Sanders, b. 1938
American basketball player